Everything I Needed to Know About Preaching

But No One Told Me!

Copyright permissions:

Unless otherwise stated, all scripture quotations taken from the New King James Bible - Copyright 1979, 1980, 1982, 1983, 1985, 1990, by Thomas Nelson Inc. Used by permission.

Other Works by Stephen Olar

Bible Studies:

The Bible School Dropout's Bigger and Better Guide to Bible Study - Print and E-book editions available.

The Bible School Dropout's Guide to More Bible Study – Print and E-book editions available

The Bible School Dropout's Guide to Building the Word of God in My Life - Print and E-book editions available

The Bible School Dropout's Guide to Hebrews

The Bible School Dropout's Guide to Dispensationalism

The Bible School Dropout's Book of Charts

The Bible School Dropout's Guide to Genesis 1-11

The Bible School Dropout's Guide to Genesis 12-26

Core Elements – Print and E-book editions available

In Hot Pursuit: Twelve Things God Wants Us To Pursue – Print and E-Book versions.

Xtreme Xianity – Print and E-Book editions available

The Name of the Lord is... Volume one: Pretty Awesome, Great, Glorious and Like Totally Excellent! - Print and E-book editions available

The Name of the Lord is... Volume Two: Hi! I'm God - Print and E-book editions available

The Name of the Lord is... Volume 2.5: Hi! I'm Still God - Print and E-book editions available

Novels:

Free – Print and E-book editions available

Icthus – Print and E-book editions available

Table of Contents

Everything I Needed to Know About Preaching but No One Told Me!

Preface

The evening services at my Church are rather informal. We meet in the fellowship hall of the chapel instead of the auditorium. We gather around tables where bowls of popcorn have been placed. There is a table of goodies people bring to munch on and there is a selection of tea, coffee and water to drink.

We have a time of singing, a time of prayer and a short message. Men of the Assembly take turns speaking at this service. They range from younger to older, less spiritually mature to more. Some have had extensive experience speaking in public and others have not. But all have something to share which the Lord has laid upon their heart.

Some are successful at getting their message across and some not so much. As a listener, sometimes the message is lost due to poor planning and execution. Sometimes it's the delivery, a person is monotone or has mannerisms which are distracting, an unclear or non-existent outline to inconsistencies in interpretation of the passage.

Ironically, while I am perfectly willing to be critical I am reminded I was once in the same place. Young and fresh at the preaching game, making the same mistakes I see these young men, and sometimes the older ones make on a regular basis.

I am by no means immune to preaching an unsuccessful message even though I have been speaking and teaching for over 30 years. It doesn't take much to realize some of these men did not study the art of preaching – also called homiletics and its partner, hermeneutics, the science and art of biblical interpretation.

That is part of the heritage of the church I attend, which is built on people exercising their gifts and there is no division of clergy and lay-person. While some people have attended Bible institutes, colleges or seminaries, the majority of speakers have not had that type of formal training. But they have the desire to speak and share. Some of them have been gifted with a speaking gift, such as a pastor-teacher or evangelist and it shows. But like most spiritual gifts, they don't come with a manual.

So an idea formed in my head to provide some guidelines for these speakers to assist them in becoming successful. I wasn't planning to write a book on this subject; there are many books on both homiletics and hermeneutics. After all, I have enough writing projects to keep me busy for several years. However, the writer in me would not let it go. I was thinking along the lines of creating a tip sheet - you know – something that is only two or three pages.

I voiced my thoughts to one of the elders on a Sunday evening, after listening to a not so successful message. He said it sounded like a good idea. By then my idea had grown and within three days. I had a title, a book number, an outline and the cover designed.

The purpose of this book is to provide some down and dirty guidelines to get a novice preacher on track to producing a message that makes sense and reaches his or her audience. This was also a good exercise for myself as well as I was refreshed on the points of producing a good message. This is important because as we older and more experienced preachers and teachers tend to fall into habits in our preferences in speaking and presentations which can also make our messages stale.

This isn't a book on everything there is to know about preaching, but about the basics and a firm foundation upon which to build. It is a book about a combination of review and about the things I wish I knew when I started out.

I pray you will find this information useful as you use your gift to build the Church and glorify God.

Stephen Olar

September 2015

Dry Mouth, Cold Sweat, Clammy Hands and Knocking Knees

Welcome to the fine art of preaching. At least welcome to the down and dirty version of how to prepare a message.

Of course I would be remiss not to mention the butterflies (or dragon flies) flittering around in your stomach. Or outright nausea and probably hurling if you are getting ready to deliver your first sermon.

Almost all people approach public speaking with about as much enthusiasm as getting a root canal done – without anesthetic. If we are preparing to share from God's Word, there is even greater pressure to get it right.

My first message after leaving Bible school was a dismal ten minutes long. So to stretch it out a bit, I opened the floor to questions and a discussion which brought my time to a semi-respectable 20 minutes. What was unexpected was the honorarium they gave me for my time. I tried to give it back; I had never been paid to preach before.

Oh, I studied about preaching and had a few dry runs at my church which was a part of the school (and the place I grew up at), but this was the first time in a place where I was relatively unknown.

I guess they liked me enough as I spoke there many times over the next few years.

So, let's talk about what this book is not.

This is not an in depth discussion on homiletics, the theories behind the science or the many different views on what preaching is or is not. There are many fine works available if you are interested in learning more about this particular subject. I will provide a list of resources you can consult at the end of the book.

This book is not just something to read that may help you. I have included some Bible studies and other exercises to assist in developing a basic understanding of what preaching is and how to go about developing a sermon which is presentable.

This book is also not designed to take the place of more formal training or a good mentor who can guide you if this is something you feel God has called you to do. If you think you have a speaking gift, then it is your responsibility to develop that gift. Preaching is not something that just happens; it takes a lot of work and preparation. And usually gets better the more you do it because you learn what works and doesn't work.

Now let's discuss what this book is about.

I wrote this book primarily as a guide for people who have a desire to speak, but have not had formal training. I did study preaching when I was at Bible College and when I left there and went to a state college, one of the prerequisite courses was called the Fundamentals of Speech.

I have been involved in speaking to people most of my working life. Many of my jobs required me to speak to people, make public presentations (try speaking to City Council carrying a six-foot teddy bear…), teaching professionally and voluntary to preaching and now writing.

There are a lot of similarities between writing and speaking. For both mediums you have to have an idea you want to share with others. You develop your argument and present your conclusions. How many sermons have you listened to that did not make any sense? The preacher was all over the place his points didn't relate to each other or support his argument?

You walked away from that Sunday message in a mental fog, smiled politely at the preacher at the back door on the way out and politely raced towards your car.

There are expectations which need to be met in order to engage your audience. Many men, and women, learn the hard way when they first start out. I have listened to many different speakers at my church over the past couple of years. I can tell by my notes which ones held my interest and those which did not. Some of them I even wrote "FAIL" on the page and closed the notebook.

That may sound harsh, but I practically grew up in Church and have listened to thousands of sermons over the years. I know what works and what doesn't. If you go to Sunday School, morning and evening services, a Bible study or two or prayer meeting during the week, and a couple of retreats a year, you get good at picking out the good messages and those which turn every minute till 12 seem like eight or nine hours.

This book is designed to take you on a step by step process to create a working outline which you will be able to use to deliver your message. It contains types of messages and examples for you to examine and work on as well as tips for producing effective visual aids and help in your delivery.

If you work through the exercises, by the end of this guide you will have the basic tools to preach. The rest is up to you.

One

Homiletics 101

It is ironically true and somewhat sad when I read one of the definitions of a sermon is a "long and tedious speech (http://dictionary.reference.com/browse/sermon?s=t)."

However the sermon is only the end product of a branch of practical theology called homiletics. I like the definition of homiletics: The art of preaching.

However that is only half of the definition. The complete definition should be the art and science of preaching. Yes effective preaching is like a grand opera of beauty and vision. It paints a picture in words that lingers in the mind of the listener long after the service has ended. It is designed to challenge our minds with the truths of God's Word and to convict and encourage us to align our lives with those truths.

And then there are the preachers who are drier than the Sahara Desert in the middle of summer. They are so boring we wish we had tiny eyelid clips to keep from falling asleep. Or the message is lost in comments made by the preacher which distract us and we focus on those errors rather than the overall message. Or worse yet, the preacher is just plain wrong and loses all credibility.

So preaching is an art and the preacher the artist. The medium of his art is the spoken word.

But there is also a science to preaching. There are definite rules and guidelines to the qualifications of the preacher, the design and form of the sermon, the type and the delivery of the message.

Defining Preaching and the Preacher

The first thing we are going to do is to define biblical preaching by looking at the words that are translated preach, preaching and preacher. Complete the *Word Summaries* on the following words. The references are from Strong's Online Concordance. Numbers prefaced by an H are from the Old Testament and G are from the New Testament. (H for Hebrew and G for Greek. In case you were wondering.)

Preacher – H6953

Preacher – G2783, G2784

Preach – H7121, H1319,

Preach – G2784, G2097, G2980, G2605,

Preaching – H7150

Preaching – G2782, G2784, G2097, G2980, G1256, G3056

Let's take a closer look at the words translated Preacher. Based on your study, what or who is a preacher?

> As the members sat waiting in the new sanctuary, they heard voices over the PA system. They heard the preacher's footsteps and his voice as he greeted others.
>
> The preacher's wife, recognizing what was happening and realizing her husband's routine, made a mad dash for the door to run interference. But she never made it and the preacher continued on with his routine.
>
> Entering the men's restroom, he took care of his bodily function...and flushed!
>
> When he finally entered the sanctuary, he was greeted by a congregation of smiling faces.
>
> Lynne Mosher
>
> http://lynnmosher.com/the-mics-on/2/ - used by permission

What did they do?

Who was their audience?

What definition did you come up with after your study words translated preach?

What did you discover from the words translated preaching?

From your study of these words what were themes the preachers were preaching?

The Qualifications of the Preacher

One of the first things to establish when determining the qualifications of the preacher is his and I dare say her gifting. Let's look at some of the verses and develop a Preacher's Qualification chart.

Ecclesiastes 12:8-12. Record your findings on the *Preacher's Qualifications* chart.

What are the qualifications of the preacher in this passage?

What does the Preacher describe has his duties?

Why is this important?

Read Acts 20:18-27 and record what you think the qualifications are in this passage?

Why would these be important?

Read Ephesians 4:11-17

What is/are the qualifications listed in this passage?

Who in this passage would need to be able to preach?

Why is this important?

Everything I Needed to Know About Preaching but No One Told Me!

Read 2 Timothy 2:15

What are the qualifications necessary for a person who wants to preach?

List your findings on your *Preacher's Qualification* Chart.

Now read 2 Timothy 3:16-17. How does this verse show us the qualifications for preaching?

Enter your findings on the Preacher Qualifications chart.

Read 1 Thessalonians 2:1-12.

What are the qualifications Paul lists here? Add these to your *Preacher's Qualification* Chart.

Read James 1:22-27

What would be the qualifications for the preacher in this passage?

Why are they important?

Record your findings on the *Preacher's Qualification* Chart.

Read 1 Peter 4:10-11

What is the qualification here for a preacher? Record it on the *Preacher's Qualification* Chart.

Now it is time for you to go to work. Continue this study on the Qualifications of the Preacher. Locate five more passages regarding preaching or speaking and the qualifications of the preacher. Record the passage, what the qualifications are and why they are important.

1.

2.

3.

4.

5.

Word Summary Date of Study:

Word:	Verse:
Strong's Number:	
Definition:	
Times Used:	
Other Sources	**Definition(s)**
Other Bible References	**How Used**
Putting it My Own Words	
Takeaway	

Word Summary   Date of Study:

Word:	Verse:
Strong's Number:	
Definition:	
Times Used:	

Other Sources	Definition(s)

Other Bible References	How Used

Putting it My Own Words	
Takeaway	

Word Summary Date of Study:

Word:	Verse:	
Strong's Number:		
Definition:		
Times Used:		
Other Sources	**Definition(s)**	
Other Bible References	**How Used**	
Putting it My Own Words		
Takeaway		

Word Summary Date of Study:

Word:	Verse:
Strong's Number:	
Definition:	
Times Used:	

Other Sources	Definition(s)

Other Bible References	How Used

Putting it My Own Words	
Takeaway	

Word Summary   Date of Study:

Word:	Verse:
Strong's Number:	
Definition:	
Times Used:	
Other Sources	**Definition(s)**
Other Bible References	**How Used**

Putting it My Own Words

Takeaway

Word Summary Date of Study:

Word:	Verse:
Strong's Number:	
Definition:	
Times Used:	

Other Sources	Definition(s)

Other Bible References	How Used

Putting it My Own Words

Takeaway

The Preacher's Qualifications

Scripture	Qualification	Defined

The Preacher's Qualifications

Scripture	Qualification	Defined

The Preacher's Qualifications

Scripture	Qualification	Defined

Additional Notes:

Additional Notes:

Two

Hermeneutics 101

Hermeneutics or biblical interpretation is another discipline in the realm of practical theology which is both an art and a science.

Bernard Ramm In his book *Protestant Biblical Interpretation* describes hermeneutics as science because it is governed by a system of rules. It is also an art because it takes skill to apply the rules correctly and not some mechanical process (Ramm).

Learning to interpret the passage you are studying in a consistent manner is vital to having a correct understanding of the passage and a message that flows naturally from Scripture.

This lesson is not going to scratch the surface of this discipline. We will be exploring some general principals regarding interpreting Scripture, but it is up to you to add some additional study on this topic. You will need to understand principles of interpreting the Word of God to be able to properly preach it.

The other premise of this lesson is my own personal bias that there is only one way to correctly interpret Scripture: Grammatical – Historical, Normal, or Literal. They are all terms which describe the same method of interpretation.

There are many misconceptions about the term "literal" with this method of interpretation. However it is only in reference to look at the passage in question the way it would have been normally viewed at the time it was written. That is the historical part of interpretation. The other part of equation is recognizing there are literary forms and devices use when something is written. That is the grammatical part of literal interpretation.

True interpretation is explained by two Latin phrases which describe early protestant interpretation. The first *is sola fidei regula* or *the only rule of faith*. This is the recognition the Bible is the only source of authority. The other phrase used is *sola scriptura* or only *Scripture* (Ramm).

In my own book *The Bible School Dropout's Bigger and Better Guide to Bible Study*, I introduced the concept of studying our Bibles the way Jesus did. When you examine how Jesus used His Bible you quickly discovered he used it in a literal sense. He did not employ a super-secret meaning to his interpretation or approached interpreting them subjectively. He took the Scriptures at face value.

This is also consistent when we look at how the other biblical writers handled the word of God (Olar, The Bible School Dropout's Bigger and Better Guide to Bible Study).

Literal interpretation is the basis for the inductive Bible study method which I have used and taught for many years.

Since I am the author and of the book and copy and paste is so much more faster than typing something original, I am including an excerpt from the book.

Use Your Bible the Way Jesus did

Does that claim sound a bit outrageous? Think about it for a moment. Who better to learn how to use your Bible by observing the one who actually authored it?

Let's take a brief look at some passages which give us insight on how Jesus used His Bible.

Matthew 4:1-11

1	The Jesus was led up by the Spirit into the wilderness to be tempted by the devil.

2	And when He had fasted forty days and forty nights, afterward He was hungry.

3	Now when the tempter came to Him, he said, If You are the Son of God, command these stones become bread.

4	But He answered and said, It is written, *Man shall not love by bread alone, but by every word that proceeds from the mouth of God*.

5	Then the devil took Him up into the holy city, set Him on the pinnacle of the temple,

6	and said to Him, If You are the Son of God, throw Yourself down, For it is written: *He shall give His angels charge over you*, and *In their hands they shall bear you up, lest you dash your foot against a stone.*

7	Jesus said to him, It is written again, You shall not tempt the LORD your God.

8	Again, the devil took Him up on an exceedingly high mountain, and showed Him all the kingdoms of the worlds and their glory.

9	And he said to Him, All these things I will give You if You will fall down and worship me.

10	Then Jesus said to him, Away with you, Satan! For it is written, You shall worship the LORD your God, and Him only you will serve.

11   Then the devil left Him, and behold, angels came and ministered to Him.

Questions for Consideration

1.   What was the passage Jesus quoted in verse 4?

2.   In the context of the original passage, what was God attempting to teach the Israelites?

3.   Did the principles from the original passage fit the circumstances in which Jesus used them?

4.   Why or why not?

5.   What was the passage Satan Quoted?

6.   Did he quote the entire passage?

7.   What part did he leave out?

8.   Did the principles from the passage in context fit the circumstances?

9.   Why or why not?

10.   How does taking the passage out of context change the meaning of the verses?

11.   When Jesus responded, what was the passage He quoted?

12.   What were the circumstances when this statement was originally made?

13.   What happened at Massah? (Hint: Exodus 17:1-7)

14.   How did the circumstances fit the situation Jesus found Himself in ?

15.   What were the last passages Jesus quoted?

16.   What was the context of those passages?

17.   How did they fit with Jesus circumstances?

18.   What is the significance of these passages and how did they apply directly to Jesus?

So....

What did we learn from how Jesus used and applied His Bible to the situation?

1.   Jesus used scriptural principles which were appropriate to His circumstances

2.   He did not take Scripture out of context, or twist them to fit the situation.

3.   He interpreted and used these passages at face value and used them in the normal sense. He didn't seek or used secondary or hidden meanings.

4.   He declared His deity in no uncertain terms and put Satan into his place.

Jesus took Scripture literally. Take a look at the passage He quoted in Synagogue?

Luke 4:16-21

16   So He came to Nazareth, where He had been brought up. And as His custom was, He went into the synagogue on the Sabbath day, and stood up to read.

17   And He was handed the book of the prophet Isaiah. And when He had opened the book, He found the place where it was written:

18   *The Spirit of the Lord* is *upon Me,*

Because He has anointed Me

To preach the gospel to the poor;

He has sent Me to heal the brokenhearted,

To proclaim liberty to the *captives*

And recovery of sight to the *blind,*

To *set at liberty those who are* oppressed;

19   *To proclaim the acceptable year of the Lord.*

20   Then He closed the book, and gave *it* back to the attendant and sat down. And the eyes of all who were in the synagogue were fixed on Him.

21   And He began to say to them, "Today this Scripture is fulfilled in your hearing."

In a very straightforward declaration, Jesus indicated the fulfillment of this prophecy made by Isaiah 800 years before occurred in the First Synagogue of Nazareth. There was nothing mystical or allegorical about what he said. He didn't expound upon some incomprehensible hidden spiritual meaning. What is interesting, however, is this is only half of the prediction.

Isaiah 61:2b-7

2b   And the day of vengeance of our God;

To comfort all who mourn,

3   To console those who mourn in Zion,

To give them beauty for ashes,

The oil of joy for mourning,

The garment of praise for the spirit of heaviness;

That they may be called trees of righteousness,

The planting of the Lord, that He may be glorified.

4   And they shall rebuild the old ruins,

They shall raise up the former desolations,

And they shall repair the ruined cities,

The desolations of many generations.

5   Strangers shall stand and feed your flocks,

And the sons of the foreigner

Shall be your plowmen and your vine dressers.

6   But you shall be named the priests of the Lord,

They shall call you the servants of our God.

You shall eat the riches of the Gentiles,

And in their glory you shall boast.

7   Instead of your shame *you shall have* double *honor,*

And *instead of* confusion they shall rejoice in their portion.

Therefore in their land they shall possess double;

Everlasting joy shall be theirs.

The remaining prediction had nothing to do with His first coming, but His second. This was often typical of Old Testament prophesies, multiple events occurring at different times seen as happening at the same time. Now, if the first half of the prophecy was literally fulfilled, what are the chances the rest will also be fulfilled literally. I'd say it's pretty good.

Jesus certainly knew His Bible. After His resurrection He walked with the two disciples returning to Emmaus, Luke 24:27 records that He went through their entire Bible, talking about the Scriptures which concerned Him. And there are a lot. Just think the first Bible study recorded in the New Testament was about Jesus. The group leader was Jesus. You can't go wrong there.

His interpretation and application of Scripture was straight to the point. Where the Pharisees had written much about the Scriptures, specifically the Law, often looking for ways to circumvent them, Jesus basically said love God first and your neighbor second - short and sweet. Too bad many preachers aren't inclined to do the same...

What about the others.....

Jesus was not the only one who used His Bible in this way. The Jewish people of Jesus day took God at His word. They believed He said what He meant and meant what He said.

- ❖ Matthew quoted Scripture to prove who Jesus was. Each passage was clear in its declaration and was understood in its normal usage.

- ❖ The disciples believed that Christ was going to set up an earthly kingdom (Acts 1:6) this is based on the promises God made in their Bible, our Old Testament.

- ❖ The Magi who came to visit Jesus were descendants from Jews who did not return after their exile and were familiar with the Jewish Scriptures. They went to Jerusalem because that is where they expected the royal baby to be. It is understandable to make such a mistake. Their people had gone into exile before Micah had prophesied the location.

- ❖ The scribes located the birthplace because it had been record by the profit Micah 800 years earlier.

- ❖ Even the Pharisees were literal in their interpretation of Scripture. They believed the Messiah and kingdom would be fulfilled as promised by Jehovah in the Old Testament. Jesus did not rebuke them for their interpretation, only for their legalism, pride and hypocrisy.

- ❖ When Paul was in the city of Berea, The Jews turned to their Scriptures to find out if he was telling the truth or blowing smoke up their tunics.

If you want to be a good preacher, whose message is consistent with the Scriptures, then it should be a priority to study hermeneutics.

In conclusion to this lesson, write a short essay – which means more than one sentence – on the connection between homiletics and hermeneutics.

Actual an essay consists of more than two sentences as well. If it has been a while, you need a thesis, introduction, arguments and conclusion. In fact, it is almost the same process for creating a message, except here you don't have to give an oral presentation on it.

The Connection between Hermeneutics and Homiletics

The Connection between Hermeneutics and Homiletics

The Connection between Hermeneutics and Homiletics

Lesson Four

Planning Your Message

So… what happens when you have an idea for a message? Do you just open your Bible and start preaching? I only know a few people who have the experience and knowledge to be able to do that.

Do you scribble down a few thoughts and desperately hope something comes together? Many aspiring preachers live in this realm of unreality. The end results are often disjointed and a waste of time for both the preacher and the audience.

Then there is the happy medium. A message that is the end result of careful preparation which will speak to both the preacher and his or her audience. I can tell you from personal experience an audience will figure out if you are prepared to preach or not and it is in the first couple of minutes of your message.

There are several stage involved in preparing a Sermon. The more effort you put into it will produce a better product at the end. In a perfect world you would spend at least an hour in preparation for every minute you will be preaching. So a 20 minute message should take 20 hours of preparation.

Since we don't live in a perfect world you can expect to spend 5-8 hours minimum in preparing your message; a message that will last anywhere from 20-45 minutes. After 45 minutes you will start to lose your audience. The human mind is designed to accept only so much information before it has to process it into long-term memory.

Preparing a message consists of three parts: 1) tell them what you are going to tell them, 2) tell them and 3) tell them what you've told them. The oral presentation consists of an Introduction (see step 1), the body of your message (step 2) and finish with an application (step 3).

Ah, if it were only that simple.

Before you get to that point there is a lot of preparation involved. The writing process consists of planning, writing and completing. If you wanted to know how to manage your time in preparing a sermon, about 50% of your efforts should be focused on the planning stage, 25% in writing the message and 25% in completing your message.

Planning

There are several step involved in the planning.   The usual steps include but are not limited to: declaring the title, deciding on the text, developing the thesis, determining the desired audience response, designing an irresistible introduction, delivering an irresistible argument and disclosing an invitation to respond to your message.

Declaring the Title

Although placed first in the list here the title of your message may not be the first, second or even the third thing you do when planning a sermon. While many people start with a title, many will wait for the title of their message until after they have developed the theme, part way through the body of the message or even wait until they have completed the message. There are no hard and fast rules in creating a title. The rule of thumb is to have it relate in some way to the message theme.

You make think that is a no brainer but how many sermons have you listened to where there was no title or the title did not relate to what the preacher's message was about. What happens? You spend half the time wondering what the title has to do with the message and the other half playing with your cell phone because you have no idea what the preacher is talking about and are too polite to interrupt him – or her as the case may be.

Deciding on the Text

When you prepare a sermon, the first thing to decide upon it the text you are preaching from. The text can consist of a verse or portion of one, a passage or a selection of verses, it is important to record them as you are basing your message on it

Alfred P. Gibbs in *The Preacher and His Preaching* indicates the word text comes from the Latin *textus* and actually means something woven (Gibbs, The Preacher and His Preaching). If we complete the analogy, the Scripture passage is the warp or the threads upon which the message or weft is run through and woven into a beautiful sermon.

I like this weaving illustration because it is a reminder our message is based on the Authority of God's Word.

The text also serves the purpose of keeping the preacher on track. The message should always be created with the verse or verses it is based on. Think about the times when you listened to a preacher start out with his chosen passage, then went on to another passage and never came back to the text of the message. It is one thing to use other passages as support or illustrations, but when you go off the track it is your audience which gets derailed.

The text also serves the role of setting your audience expectations. They read the title of your Sermon in the bulletin (if there is one) and see the text. Some of them may look up the passage if it is listed and this starts the process of the audience beginning to buy into your message.

Keeping focus on your text will help you to keep focused on your theme, which is the next thing you want to write down.

Developing the Thesis

Ever listen to a sermon, or a speech, and have no clue what the message was about? Yeah, we've all been there. Probably you have preached a sermon like that. It is actually a common mistake when a person is starting out. Some experienced preachers have been guilty of the same thing. We preach a message which left the audience scratching their heads... well maybe an inside head scratch because they are still in church with you and are too polite to tell you your message made no sense to them and had to entertain themselves by playing on their cell phones.

The thesis is the theme of your message. This is also called the hypothesis or argument. The thesis statement presents your premise or argument in a clear and concise statement. Let me repeat that last part for emphasis: CLEAR AND CONCISE STATEMENT.

The goal is to create one crystal clear sentence which explains what your message is about. In the odd message or two it is acceptable to use two sentences. But that is only rarely and if you have to use two sentences, you probably have enough material to create two messages.

Determining the Intended Audience Response

Before you put your argument together, you need to determine what you want your audience to do when you have presented your message. Is the intent of your message to simply provide knowledge? (Not on the top of my list.) Do you want them to go home, pull out their Bibles and study what you have presented? Or do you want them to run up the aisles of the church, tears running down their faces as they repent of their sins and fall at the altar pouring out their lives to God?

Now don't get me wrong. Knowledge is a good thing. After all, that is an important part of your message; providing knowledge on the passage which you want to talk about it. I think that aim is incomplete. You want to challenge them to accept your message and incorporate the truth you have been proclaiming into their lives.

Normal types of writing and speaking often present options to the audience. However, God is into changing lives in a positive and meaningful way. This is an important aspect to consider as you develop your message.

Designing an Irresistible Introduction

Whether your audience stays with you and considers your message depends largely on your introduction. If you start off flat, then the audience gets the ideas the message to follow will also be flat. They have mentally checked out and are too polite to get up and walk out.

Your introduction serves three purposes: 1) Captures your audience's attention, 2) Builds your credibility, and 3) Previews your message (Thill, Bovee and Cross).

The introduction sets the tone of the message and you want to capture your audience's attention. Gibbs describes the introduction as the porch of the house or the dawning sun of a new day. It gives a hint of what is to come (Gibbs, The Preacher and His Preaching).

There are several ways you can capture your audience's attention.

They include:

- ❖ Uniting your audience around a common goal.
- ❖ Asking a question to pique their interest.
- ❖ Use humor.
- ❖ Tell a relevant story.
- ❖ State some startling statistic.
- ❖ Conduct an activity related to your theme.

And introduction also serves the purpose of helping your audience understand the content and structure of your message. You can summarize the main point of your message, identify your major points and indicate in which order you will be expanding on these points (Thill, Bovee and Cross).

So step one in the prewriting process – tell them what you are going to tell them, is complete.

The introduction also gives you a chance to establish your credibility. Now you may asking isn't that a contradiction of what I stated earlier? After all I am speaking on the authority of God's Word.

Absolutely.

Let me remind you of a couple of verses you looked at in an earlier chapter. Complete a *Verse Summary* on them.

2 Timothy 2:15

2 Timothy 3:16, 17

1 Peter 4:11

According to these verses how do you establish your credibility on the basis of the authority of God's Word?

During the introduction you can also build credibility by telling people who you are (especially if speaking to a new audience), why you are there and How your audience will benefit from listening to you.

Delivering an Irresistible Argument

It is now time to deliver the goods. You have introduced your topic. The audience sits primed and ready to give you a listen. Don't drop the ball. Most messages consist of three to five points carefully selected and arranged to prove the argument you are going to make. If you have more than five you have enough material for two messages.

Every point you make in the body of your sermon is designed to do one thing: support your thesis or theme and prepare the audience to accept your conclusions in the application portion of the message.

Your written message should look like this

Thesis or theme:

Introduce the theme:

1.   Point one argument in support of your theme.

     A. Supporting material for point one.

     B. Supporting material for point one.

     C. Etc.

2.   Point two argument to support your theme.

     A. Supporting material for point two.

     B. Etc.

3.   Get the picture?

Now let's take a look at a couple of sermons in the Bible and complete an *Outline Summary* for them. You may not be able to fill in all the information on the chart, like a title, but you should be able to discover the theme and the arguments the preacher used to develop and support his thesis.

Ecclesiastes 2:1-11

Acts 17:22-32

A great part in the success of your sermon is sticking to your outline like a fly in a fly trap. As you are presenting your argument to your audience you are also building the case for them to accept your argument and respond accordingly.

This is the part of the message in which you have told them.

Disclosing an Invitation to Respond to Your Message

Finally you are going to tell your audience what you have just told them.

A successful conclusion, for the world of preaching, is to recap your theme and major points. Now this is where you issue what you want the audience to do. Near the beginning you should have stated what the intended response of your audience should be.

Now you lay it out for them. The goal of a good message should include the sharing of knowledge and educating the customer, but you want to encourage them to examine your presentation of the truth with the goal in mind to accept it and move to incorporate into their lives.

Some preachers issue an "Altar call" at the end of the message. To come forward to kneel at front of the church to demonstrate God has been working in your life. Others, depending on the tradition of the church, may ask you to raise your hand at the closing prayer or ask the audience to speak with someone later.

The word *conclusion* should be an important reminder that you are ending your message. Don't you find it annoying when a preacher concludes his message several times? After the third "and in conclusion" you realized the roast is going to burn if you don't leave in the next thirty seconds and you have company coming.

Gibbs said, "The speaker's concluding point should coincide with his stopping point."

And in Conclusion...

You should have noticed there are a couple of extra Sermon notes in this lesson.

Your assignment is to listen to a couple of messages, preferably by different speakers and see if you can determine if they are successful in presenting their message. I encourage you to start bringing a notebook with you to Church to take notes on the message. One, it helps you to retain the points of the sermon and two, it makes it easier to analyze the message and to actually consider the application the preacher made.

If you want to be used of God as a great preacher you should listen to and read sermons by contemporary preachers and by the classical greats.

All done for now…

Verse Summary

Date of Study:

Title:	
Verse:	
Strong's Number and Definition(s)	**Used Elsewhere**
Quotation? Yes No	**Summary of Original Passage**
Summary of Verse in Context	
Putting it in My Own Words	
Takeaway	

Verse Summary   Date of Study:

Title:	
Verse:	
Strong's Number and Definition(s)	**Used Elsewhere**
Quotation? Yes No	**Summary of Original Passage**

Summary of Verse in Context

Putting it in My Own Words

Takeaway

Sermon Notes

Speaker:	Date:	Location :

Scripture:	Title:	

Theme: (Purpose or goal of the message)	

Verse:	Point:	Message Notes:	Reference:

Takeaway:

Sermon Notes

Speaker:		Date:		Location :	
Scripture:		Title:			
Theme: (Purpose or goal of the message)					
Verse:	Point:	Message Notes:			Reference:
Takeaway:					

Sermon Notes

Speaker:	Date:		Location :
Scripture:	Title:		
Theme: (Purpose or goal of the message)			

Verse:	Point:	Message Notes:	Reference:

Takeaway:

Sermon Notes

Speaker:		Date:		Location :	
Scripture:		Title:			
Theme: (Purpose or goal of the message)					
Verse:	Point:	Message Notes:			Reference:

Takeaway:

Sermon Notes

Speaker:		Date:	Location :
Scripture:		Title:	
Theme: (Purpose or goal of the message)			
Verse:	**Point:**	**Message Notes:**	**Reference:**

Takeaway:

Additional Notes:

Additional Notes:

Additional Notes:

Lesson Five

Writing Your Message

Now that you have done all of your prewriting exercises: Psych! There is still one more piece to the prewriting preparation before you actually start developing your message in earnest.

What type of sermon are you preaching?

Type? You mean there is more than one approach to preaching a sermon?

Yup!

Depending on which expert (or web site) you are reading there are four to ten sermon types. Some authors combined a couple or did not include them. The following chart explains the type, its advantages and disadvantages. I've also included sample outlines for you to examine.

Type	Definition	Advantages	Disadvantages
Personal Testimony	Telling your personal experience/salvation story. Suitable for preaching to a first time audience.	-It is a natural place to start. -People like stories -is prominent in Scriptures.	-easy to embellish -self-promotion -think it has no value -downplay Christ or the Scriptures
Textual	The Sermon theme and outline is based upon the text.	-The Scripture is prominent -Makes for variety	-The Bible can appear as a book of isolated texts -the overall unity is not apparent
Topical	Deciding on a topic and Compiling Scripture from several passages	-Demonstrates More of the Bible's unity -Can allow for an in depth discussion	-The Bible is not a compilation of topics -The Preacher will run out of topics
Textual – Topical	This is a combination where the message is developed by the text and the topic	-utilizes a strong biblical base -allows for freedom of development -can allow for an in depth discussion	-The issues are similar to those of the textual and topical sermons.

Type	Definition	Advantages	Disadvantages
Expository	Focuses on explaining a passage of Scripture in its context. The passage is interpreted, amplified and applied.	-It places emphasis totally on the authority of God's Word. -It emphasizes the unity of Scripture. -With 66 books, the preacher will never run out of material	-can degenerated into a disconnected collection of sermonettes with no connection to a central theme -become a running commentary. -can by dry if presented incorrectly
Doctrinal	The teaching of theological subjects, doctrinal statements, denominational distinctions and Christian beliefs with the goal of gaining understanding and acceptance.	-Lays out a systematic progression of what and why we believe a certain teaching. -One of the major reasons the Word Exists (2 Timothy 3:16)	-can be dry -hard to make personal applications
Historical	The study of a historical biblical incident and drawing out spiritual applications.	-Similar to an expository message. -Everyone loves a good story	-Over spiritualizing the incident. -Creating an extreme application that is not supported in the context of Scripture.
Biographical	Similar to a historical sermon except studying a person instead	-Human interest in reading about people; their struggles, failures and victories.	-Similar to historical sermons.
Ethical	Messages dealing with Christian living in personal and social situations.	-Provides a biblical basis for how we are to live according to God's standards	-Can degenerate into a person's moral viewpoint with little Scriptural support.
Special Programs	Messages geared to holidays or promoting a specific program or ministry	-Designed for setting and promoting priorities for church growth and direction.-Celebrate holidays like Easter and Christmas.	-Can be viewed as a money-grabbing scheme or someone's personal agenda

(Gibbs, The Preacher and His Preaching), (Broadus, On the Preparation and Delivery of Sermons, 4th ed.), (Blackwood)

Personal Testimony

Title:	Topic:
Saul the Terrorist	The conversion of Saul

Scripture:	Theme:
Acts 9:1-30 cf Acts 22:1-16; Acts 25:12-18; Galatians 1:11-24	Jesus is in the Business of Changing Lives

Key words/phrases:

Verses	Points	Support/illustrations
	Introduction: Interview with a terrorist.	Acts 7:54-8:3
	- Interviewed many interesting people – The most interesting was a former terrorist – Who became a Baptist preacher. - God is in the business of changing lives – and chooses a wide variety of people with different backgrounds. - Saul was a terrorist in his day –	
	1. On the Road To Damascus	
	A. Chains, Shackles and Chains	
	B. Blinded by the Light	
9:1-9	2. In Damascus	
	A. Why Me Lord?	
	B. The Baptism	
9:10-22	C. I Am No Longer the Same	
	3. You Are Now Leaving Damascus	
	A. A Tisket, a Tasket, Paul is in a Basket.	

9:23-30	B. Suspicion C. Paul's Got a Brand New Bag.	

Takeaway
Application: - It doesn't matter who you are, what age you are or what you have done, Jesus died for you and has a plan. If He can take a former terrorist and change the world, what will he do for you?

Textual Outline (Gibbs, The Preacher and His Preaching)

	Title: The Gospel in Seven Words	
Scripture: Ephesians 2:8	Theme (Context): Salvation originates from God's grace and experienced on the condition of faith	
Key Words and phrases		
By grace are you saved by faith		

Verse	Points	Support
	1. By Grace – the Source	
	a. It's definition	
	b. It' origin	
	c. It's manifestation	1Peter 5:10
		John 1:17
	2. Are – the Certainty	2 Corinthians 8:9
	a. A present salvation	
	b. An assured salvation	
	c. A contrasted salvation	John 3:19
		2 Corinthians 4:3
	3. You – the Object	
	a. Dead	Ephesians 2:1-3
	b. Deluded	
	c. Disobedient	
	d. Defiled	John 5:24
	e. Darkened	Romans 6:14
	f. Doomed	Revelation 21:27
	4. Condition – Saved	

	a. From sin's penalty b. From sin's power c. From sin's presence 5. Through Faith – the Medium a. Definition b. Object – Christ c. Result - Salvation	
Takeaway		

Topical Outline (Olar, The Bible School Dropout's Bigger and Better Guide to Bible Study)

Title: Remember Me	**Topic:** The Lord's Supper
Main Scripture: Matthew. 26:26-30; Mark 14:22-26; Luke 22:14-20, Acts 2:42-46; 20:7; 1 Corinthians 10:15-22; 11:11-26	**Theme:** The Lord's Supper is more than a 10 minute Addendum.

Key Words and phrases: remembrance, thanksgiving, communion, covenant, will not eat or drink,

Verse	Points	Cross References:
Matt 26:26	1. A Memorial	Joshua 4:1-7
Mark 14:22		1 Peter 1:18-19
Luke 22:19	1.1 a physical reminder	
1 Cor 11:24-25	1.2 His sacrifice	
	1.3 the shedding of His blood	
	1.4 the price paid for my salvation	
Matt 26:28		Jer 31:31-34
Mark 14:24	2. A New Covenant	Heb 8-9:22
Luke 22:20		Gen 9:12
1 cor 11:24-25	2.1 covenant sealed with blood	Gen 17:11
	2.1.1 Noah, Abraham, Moses (Law)	Ex 31:13
	2.2 a new one to replace the old one	
	2.3 a sign of the new covenant	
	2.3.1 Noah = rainbow, Abraham = circumcision,	

Matt 26:26-27 Mark 14:22-23 Luke 22:19-20 Acts 2:42-46 1 Cor 11:24-25	Moses = Sabbath keeping 3. A Praise 3.1 blessing (eulogeo) = to speak well of, praise, thanksgiving 3.1.1 speaking well of Christ - His sacrifice 3.1.2 speaking well of God - mercy, grace, provision of new covenant 3.2 thanksgiving (eucharisto) = expressing gratitude, 3.2.1 His sacrifice 3.2.2 the New Covenant 3.2.3 salvation 3.3 a celebration	
Acts 2:42-46 Acts 20:7-11 1 Cor 10:16-21	4. A Sharing 4.1 communion = fellowship = sharing 4.2 unity of the body 4.3 our unity in Christ 4.4 our disunity with the world 4.4.1 not to partake of the cup/table of demons unbelievers do not partake 4.4.2 not to be unequally yoked 4.5 corporate experience 4.5.1 observed every time the disciples gathered together	1 Cor 12:12-27 1 Cor 14:26 2 Cor 6:14-16

1 Cor 10: 16-18	5. A Participation	
	5.1 our privilege as a priest	Lev 7:6
	5.1.1 partake of the sacrifice	Matt 26:10
	5.2 Our offering as priests	Mark 14:6
	5.2.1 praise	Rom 12:1
	5.2.2 good works (worship?)	1 Cor 9:13
	5.2.3 sharing	1 Cor 14:26-27
	5.2.4 ourselves	Heb 13:15-16
1 Cor 11:26		1 Peter 2:9-10
	6. A Proclamation	
	6.1 of His death	Rom 3:21-26
	6.2 of the gospel	Rom 5:1
	6.3 a witness to the world of the work of Christ	1 Cor 2:1-2
Matt 26:29		1 Cor 9:14
Mark 14:25	7. An Anticipation	
Luke 22:17		
1 Cor 11:26	7.1 Jesus made a promise	Heb 10:22-23
	7.2 an act of faith	Heb 11:1
	7.3 looking to the future	Heb 11:6
1 Cor 11:17-22		
1 Cor 14:26–40	8. A Method	
	8.1 God is a God of order	1 John 1:5-10
	8.2 self-examination	

| | 8.3 how not to come together | |
| | 8.4 how to come together | |

Takeaway:

When I participate in the Lord's Supper, I am exercising my privilege of being a priest. As a priest I am also offering sacrifices of praise, thanksgiving and worship.

I am commemorating the sacrifice of Christ on the Cross and the provisions provided by the New Covenant.

By participating, I am showing the unity of the body of believers

I am declaring the Gospel and looking forward to the return of My Lord and Saviour.

Textual-Topical Outline (Broadus, On the Preparation and Delivery of Sermons, 4th ed.)

	Title: What will you do with Jesus?
Scripture: Isaiah 53:3-12	Theme (Context): He who was despised and rejected will be admired and accepted

Key Words and phrases

He is despised and rejected by men

Verses	Points	Support
Isaiah 53:3-5	1. He is despised and rejected a. despised and rejected b. a man of sorrows c. acquainted with grief d. afflicted	John 1:1-13
Isaiah 53:6-11	2. He is admired, yet rejected a. He was wounded b. He was chastised c. He was sacrificed d. He healed us	Mark 15:1-15
Isaiah 53:12	3. He will be admired and accepted a. Will receive a portion of the spoils b. Made intercessor c. Will return in triumph	Revelation 19:11-16

Takeaway

What with you do with Jesus? Despise and reject? Admire and reject? Admire and accept?

Expository Outline (Olar, The Bible School Dropout's Bigger and Better Guide to Bible Study)

Book: 1 Peter	Title: My hope is built on nothing less	
Passage: 1:1-5	Theme (Context): Our hope is built on a living saviour	
Key Words: hope, holy, salvation		Key Verse: 1:5

Verse	Points	Support
1-5	Topic one: Hope	
2	1. The Process of Salvation.	
	1.1 Chosen according to the foreknowledge of God	John 10:14,
	1.1.1 Chosen in eternity past	Ephesians 1:3-4; 2:8-9,
	1.1.2 Chosen by His grace	1 Peter 1: 15;
	1.1.3 Chosen for a purpose	2:9-10
	1.1.4 Chosen to be holy	
	1.1.5 Chosen to be a special people.	
	1.2 Set apart by the Holy Spirit	John 3:6-8
	1.2.1 A product of the Holy Spirit	1 Corinthians 12:13
	1.2.2 Drawn to the gospel	Titus 3:5
	1.2.3 Set apart to salvation	
	1.2.4 Placed in the ranks of the redeemed	
	1.2.5 Enable us to be holy because God is holy	
	1.3 Purified by the Son	Romans 5:1
3	1.3.1 Based on his obedience	Galatians 4:4-5

4	1.3.2 When He shed his blood	Hebrews 9:12-14
	2. The Results of Salvation	1 Cor. 15:12-19
	2.1 Based on the resurrection of Jesus	John 17:22-24
	2.2 An inheritance	Hebrews 8:15-17
	2.3 Not capable of corruption	1 Peter 1:23
	2.4 Undefiled	
5	2.5 Does not fade away	
	2.6 Kept for me in Heaven	
	3. The Completion of Salvation.	John 10:28
	3.1 Guarded by God	
	3.2 Kept through faith	
	3.3 Kept until Jesus returns	

Take Away
God the Father saved me when he chose me, Jesus saved me when he died on the cross. The Holy Spirit saved me when I confessed Jesus. God has given me hope in my salvation.

Doctrinal Outline

	Title: The Inspiration of The Bible
Scripture: 2 Timothy 3:14-17	Theme (Context): The Bible originated with God and is His communication with me
Key Words and phrases	

Verses	Points	Support

2 Timothy 3:16	1. The Bible proclaims its own authority
	
	a. Inspiration" is a translation of Greek word *theopneustos*
	    (1) *Theopneustos* is derived from two Greek words
	        (a). *theos* = "God"
	        (b). *pneo* = "to blow, to breathe"
	    (2). Means "God-breathed"
	
	"God-breathed" conveys idea of God-originated
	
	c. Belief in Scripture is necessary and commanded
	    (1) Christ indicated the Pharisees realy didn't believe the Word.
	
	    (2) Paul said his words were the Lord's commandments
	
	d. God has promised to preserve His word for His people in all generations
	    (1) His Word shall not depart
	
	    (2) Christ came to fulfill the Law (OT)
	
	    (3) Scripture cannot be broken
	
	e. The New Testament writers and Jesus all referred to the Old Testament as authoritative
		
		John 5:46-47
		
		I Corinthians 14:36-38
		
		Isaiah 59:21
		
		Matthew 5:17-18
		John 10:35

	(1) Jesus	
	(2) Phillip	
	f. The New Testament claims the same authority for itself as the Old Testament	Like24:13-27 Acts 8:26-37
		2 Peter 3:14-16
	2. Bible was given to us for:	
	a. Making us wise for salvation through faith	Ephesians 2:8-9
	b. Doctrine	2 Timothy 2:15
	-Teaching us God's way	Hebrews 4:12
	c. Reproof	
	-When we get off of the way	
	d. Correction	
	- How to get back on the path	

Takeaway

The Bible originated with God, and I can have complete confidence in it. It provides the message of salvation and how God expects me to live.

Biographical Outline (Olar, The Bible School Dropout's Bigger and Better Guide to Bible Study)

Person: Mary B	Title: X-treme X-tianity!
Scripture: Matthew 26:1-13; Mark 14:1-9; Luke 10:38-42; John 11:1-46, 12:1-6	Theme (Context): Being an extreme Christian begins at the feet of Jesus
Key Words and phrases	

Verse	Points	Support

Luke 10:38-42	I. Extreme Devotion- sitting at the feet of Jesus
	
	A. Going against convention
	
	   -Mary was expected to be in the kitchen, not out with the guys.
	
	B. A matter of priorities
	
	   -she wanted to know Jesus
	
	   -she wanted to learn
		Matt 6:33
		
		Psalm 42:1-2
		
		2 Timothy 2:25
		
		Philippians 3:7-13

John 11:28-38	II. Extreme Faith - falling at the feet of Jesus A. A testing of our faith B. Jesus calls to us in our pain C. He feels our pain D. He cares deeply E. He rewards our faith	Hebrews 4:4-14, 11:1-3 1 Peter 5:7 Jer 31:13
John 12:2-8 Matthew 26:1-13 Mark 14:1-9	III. Extreme Worship - anointing the feet of Jesus A. Worship costs	2 Samuel 24:24 Rom 12:1-2

	B. Worship is an intimate experience	
	C. Worship lingers after the act is complete	
	D. Worship is honouring	

Takeaway

3 steps to being an extreme Christian:

1. Devotion - Focus totally on Jesus

2. Faith - Put your complete trust in Jesus

3. Worship - Give your all to Jesus.

The more time I spend learning about Jesus, the more I am able to trust him and acknowledge Him for who He is and what He has done for me.

Historical Outline (Olar, The Bible School Dropout's Bigger and Better Guide to Bible Study)

Title: Passover: Deliverance by Blood		
Main Scripture: Exodus 11-12:1-30	**Topic:** The Passover	
Key Words and phrases:		

Verse	Points	Support
11:1-10	A. Announcement of Judgment - one more plague - favour granted to the Israelites to gain silver and gold - details of the judgment - announcement made to Pharaoh - Pharaoh's rejection	
12:1-11	B. Institution of Passover - God gives instructions - lamb sacrificed at sunset - lamb to roasted whole, no bones to be broken - the entire lamb was to be eaten	Psalm 34:20 1 Corithians 5:7
12:12-13	- blood to be spattered on the door posts and lintel - Children of Israel to be prepared to move on God's command C. Deliverance by Blood	Hebrews 11: 28

		2 Peter 3:9
		Romans 5:9
12:14-28	- at midnight God will pass through the land and strike the firstborn.	
	- the only exception was on those who believed God and had blood sprinkled on the doorposts	
	- God promised He would pass over those houses	
		Luke 22:19-20
	D. Memorial of Deliverance	
12:29-30	- the feast to be a perpetual memorial - God declared it an everlasting ordinance	
	- Tied with the feast of unleavened bread	
	- instructions repeated	
		Rev 20:11-14
	E. Judgment Falls	
	- As God promised, death came to the first born at midnight	
	-none were exempt from Pharaoh to servants to livestock	

Takeaway
- the only people who were saved were those who believed God
- no one was exempt from judgment
- God kept His promise of deliverance
- pictures the sacrifice of Jesus - Paul calls him our passover, sacrificed for us
- When God sees the blood of Christ applied to us, we are saved from His wrath and judgment

Ethical Outline (Copeland)

Moral Authority	**Title:** The Bible: the authority on moral issues.	
Scripture: 2 Timothy 3:16-17; various	**Theme (Context):** When it comes to making decisions on moral issues, the Word of God stand as the final authority.	
Key Words and phrases		
Not applicable		
Verses	**Points**	**Support**
	Introduction 1. Many conflicting views and different opinions on what is right and wrong. 2. Traditional moral values constantly being challenged 3. Standards of morality are often subjective – no absolute truth or values 4. The Bible stands for absolute truth and should be the basis for our moral positions A. Accepted Authorities in Morality 1. "If it feels good, it must be right." - The Bible warns against trusting feelings. 2. "Let your conscience be your guide." -Paul served God with a good conscience – even when he was persecuting Christians. 3. "All my friends are doing it."	 Proverbs 28:26 Jeremiah 10:23 Proverbs 14:12 Acts 23:1; 29:9-11

	-Jesus describes the consequences of being in the majority -Would have drowned in Noah's day -Israel wandered in the desert for 40 years	Matthew 7:13-14
	4. "The minister/pastor/elder says it's ok." - "Men of God" would not lead people astray. In the Bible religious leaders have been called 1) The blind leading the blind 2) Minsters of Satan 3) False teachers	Matthew 15:12-14 2 Corinthians 11:13-15
	B. God's standards	2 Peter 3:1-3,12-15,17-19
	1. The Bible 2. Jesus 3. Apostles	2 Timothy 3:16-17 Matthew 28:18 John 14:26; 16:12-13
	Conclusion	1 Thessalonians 4:1-8 Ephesians 4:17-32
	Christians have the authority on moral issues 1. In Jesus 2. In God 3. In His Word	

Takeaway

When taking a stand on a moral issue, I need to make sure my stand is made on the authority of God's Word – the Bible.

Event Outline

Thanksgiving	**Title:** Thank God and Remember	
Scripture: Various	**Theme (Context):** Thanksgiving is a remembrance of the blessings God has bestowed upon us.	
Key Words and phrases		
Verses	**Points**	**Support**
Psalm 30:4	1. Give thanks and remember his holiness	
Psalm 75:1	2. Give thanks and remember his works	
Psalm 77:11	3. Give thanks and remember His wonders	
1 Corinthians 11:23-26	4. Give thanks and remember His covenant	
Takeaway		
What has God done in your life that you are thankful for?		

You should have had an opportunity to at least glance at each of the outlines demonstrating the various sermon types. There are more sermons types out there, but I have to end this chapter at some point, not totally confuse you and create some exercises to tie it all up in a pretty bow.

You will notice they outlines generally follow the pattern we discussed in the previous Chapter. So there is a thesis, proposition or argument. Then there is an introduction which introduces the theme. The outline presents the major support for the theme and then there are sub points under each point.

The outlines end with a conclusion which sums up the points and brings us back to our theme. These outlines also include a take away which is the point you want your audience to consider and act upon.

Wait a minute... not all these outlines have all that information in them. So what's up with that?

Well what's up is it is your assignment to go over the outlines and add the missing elements. Some of these outlines are missing an introduction. Some of them don't have any sub points or are missing a conclusion.

You will also have to support your sub points with Scripture and tie them into the arguments already showing in the outlines. Support can also include a story or other illustration you may have. We have not touched on this part to writing your message. That will be covered in the next couple of lessons.

By the time you are finished with this chapter, you should have a good general idea on how to create a message which is well on its way to reaching your intended audience in the way you have planned.

Additional Notes:

Additional Notes:

Lesson Six

Completing Your Message

The third stage is called the completing phase. Whether you are planning to read your message word for word, have a basic outline or are going to wing it, you still need to make sure your message is presentable to your audience.

In this part of the writing process you will evaluate the content of your message, reviewing it to make sure you're points are supporting your thesis and it is organized to deliver maximum impact.

Some of the things you should pay attention to include:

Fact Checking

When you go over your message the first thing you want to do is make sure you have all the facts straight. Double check your references to make sure they are the correct ones. Yeah, we've all been there. We are into our message and we turn to the passage we are talking about or using as an illustration and Voila! It is the wrong reference. We were rushing to get it done because we had to preach in 30 minutes, were distracted by the phone, the dog barking, the kids fighting or any one of a hundred reasons. But whatever the reason, we wrote down the wrong verse.

We break out in a cold sweat while we fumble around our Bible looking for the right one. Forget it, if you can't recover in a few seconds, swallow your losses (and pride) and move on.

While you are checking facts, also make sure you are referring to the correct passage of Scripture. I was listening to a message one evening. The speaker's text was in Jeremiah 31 and referred to the fulfilment of this in Matthew 2 when Jesus and His family return from exile in Egypt. Well he was half right. Jeremiah 31 contains a prophecy which is fulfilled in Matthew 2 – but it was in reference to massacre of the children in Bethlehem by Herod. The passage referring to God calling His Son out of Egypt is from Hosea, not Jeremiah.

It doesn't sound like such a big deal. But if a person is aware of the error and the preacher is not or does not correct it, speaks to the credibility of the speaker as the "product" specialist. When one mistake is noticed, the message gets lost as the listener attempts to determine if there are other mistakes as well.

A friend of mine was teaching a children's Sunday school class shortly after she had become a Christian. She misunderstood a prophecy of the passage and told the kids just how more violent the crucifixion was – she told her class the Romans broke every bone in Jesus' body. The Bible teaches the opposite occurred (Psalm 34:20). When the Romans went to break Jesus' legs to speed up the death process, they discovered He had already died.

While you are checking your references ensure your other points are also correct. The speaker who indicated the New American Standard version was the most literal English translation available probably was not acquainted with Young's Literal Translation. People who bestow the more literal translation title to The King James or New King James versions would not be impressed with such a statement either.

Such claims should not be made without some sort of qualification, preferably another qualified source than yourself. The phrase "In my opinion," should not be in your vocabulary. Other people have an opinion just as valid as yours. Unless you're audience is on the same page as you, it's best to avoid such statements.

If you are using historical illustrations you want to make sure these facts are correct: dates, people, places, and the actual events. You can bet on someone in your audience will know that you made a mistake and may even share that with you. More than likely people will no longer pay attention to the main point of your message but start listening for more errors.

Clarity

I usually laugh when I see "fail" memes on Face Book. The message on a church sign read "Having trouble sleeping? We have sermons, come hear one." Did draw a chuckle, but as I thought about it there was a truth to it which had nothing to do with encouragement and hope.

We can assume the person who put up the sign was thinking the messages they preach can bring peace of mind, but in reality, it unfortunately reflects many Sunday morning messages: they will put you to sleep.

Clarity in your preaching is a must if you want to effectively communicate to your audience.

For some strange reason, many scholarly people and preachers like to use big words in their messages. I'm not sure if it is because they want to sound "religious" or don't really know what they are talking about and want to keep their audience confused. You want to make sure theological terms are defined for both yourself and your audience. If you are unsure of the meaning of a word, you can be sure your audience will figure that out and will not buy into your premise.

When you read through your message, or outline, also make a point to use words which are three syllables or less. The longer the word, the more distracting it is to the audience. You want them to consider your message not think about unfamiliar words. They will stop thinking about your message and start thinking about Sunday dinner.

Often what looks good on paper does not necessarily translate well to oral presentation. If you are planning to write out and read your message word for word, then practice out loud so you can check the flow. Also, see if you are correctly pronouncing unfamiliar words. Your audience will become distracted if you pronounce them wrong or put the emphasis on the wrong syllable.

Illustrations

There was a Bible College student who once had the opportunity to visit with Ruth Bell Graham. Hoping to glean some words of wisdom from the wife of the world's best known evangelist and preacher, Billy Graham, he asked her for some advice about preaching. Her response was threefold: "Preach expository sermons, keep it short and use lots of illustrations. (Morgan)"

The best remembered sermons are not those which the preacher throws out verse after verse, but those which are filled with illustrations and stories. When a spiritual truth is illustrated by a story, we are more inclined to remember the point the speaker is attempting to make because we can relate the message to something that may have happened to us, or we can see how this truth can be played out in real life. Successful preachers, teachers and public speakers know the value of using stories to help their audience understand their message and to motivate them to action (Olar, The Bible School Dropout's Guide to More Bible Study).

In The *Preacher and His Preaching*, Haddon W. Robinson stated an illustration "needs to be exactly on target so that listeners grasp the meaning in a flash without explanation. (Robinson)"

Illustrations serve several purposes. The primary function is to support your argument. Others include assisting the audience in understanding the message, give them something to think about, help explain difficult passages and enforce the truth of Scripture. It is important for the preacher to be like Jesus when He said many times, "The kingdom of heaven is like…" Use a lot of "likes" in your message (Gibbs, The Preacher and His Preaching, 6th ed.).

Other reasons to use illustrations are to capture your audience's attention, evoke an emotional response and proving your argument (Broadus, On the Prepartion and Delivery of Sermons, 4th ed.).

Illustrations come in many shapes. They can include:

1. Anecdotes: An Anecdote is a short account of an incident or event. They can be made up, a personal account or a third party story. Often they are humorous but they are designed to support your argument.

2. Scripture: Yes you can use other passages to illustrate and support your message.

3. Quotations: Quotations are powerful illustrations when you use them in any part of your message. They add strength to your argument and add to its credibility by way of a third party.

4. Poetry: A preacher may use a poem or part of a song to illustrate his or her message. Most often used in the introduction or conclusion of the message the right phrase can crystalize the truth you are trying to communicate.

5. Nature: Job 12:7-8 and 1 Corinthians 11:14 tell us that nature around us proves God's truths: so do Psalm 19 and Romans 1:20.

6. Historical events: Even going back into Scripture or from other historical sources you can discover excellent illustrations which can portray the truth in your message and support your argument.

7. Visualization: Many preachers will open their message with the phrase, "Picture this." It will get the audience thinking about the main point of your message as you present your argument.

8. Questions: Especially in the conclusion a well thought out question will target the specific goal you have in mind for your audience to consider. Many people do not think of questions as illustrations but if you consider you are including information to support your thesis, a question fits the purpose of an illustration.

9. Prayer: When not used to summarize the sermon or repeat the application word for word can be used as an illustration when concluding your message. An earnest prayer to for the leading of the Spirit in bringing clarity, a plea for action on the hearers' (including the preacher's) minds and hearts is a powerful tool. You are turning the outcome of your sermon totally over to God's control to act upon the audience.

Putting it into Practice

Look over the sermon outlines from the last chapter and use some of the suggestions we have discussed here. Check to make sure the Scripture passages mentioned support the argument. Are the outlines themselves clear in their logical progression?

Finally make some notes on the outlines as to what kind of illustrations you would use to further support the argument. If you are preparing a message already then apply what we have talked about to your outline.

If you are not in a group working on this study or being mentored, used one of your trusted friends to look at your outline and ask for feedback. Make sure they are specific as friends don't want to hurt your feelings and tell you it is good when it really isn't.

In the next lesson we will be looking at presentation aids, like handouts and electronic media, such as PowerPoint and Prezzi. If you don't know what a Prezzi is, you will…

Additional Notes:

Lesson Seven

Effective Visuals

The cliché "A picture is worth a thousand words" is never truer when it comes to choosing visual effects for your message.

When the speaker thinks about visuals electronic presentations like PowerPoint immediately come to mind. If you are more old-school you may remember things like overhead projectors, white or black boards, slides and flip charts. Until the church I grew up in installed a projector there was a white board behind the pulpit.

Often the speaker would be holding a white board marker in his hand as he wrote out the points of his message or put up answers provided by the audience in an ongoing discussion. Now this was more common during the Sunday school session than the worship session, but the board was frequently used for both.

The title of this chapter is called Effective Visuals for a very important reason – because there are such things as ineffective visuals which distract your audience instead of helping them understand and accept your argument.

Equipment

When deciding on visuals the first factor is the size of the audience or room. If your audience is less than 50 people, then a white board or flip chart can be effective, especially if you are initiating a discussion, looking to record responses to your questions, setting up a group exercise or illustrating a difficult concept.

In a large space or a larger group of people, these tools are not as effective as the further away you get from the podium the harder it gets to see what's written.

Almost extinct are overhead projectors... at least the standalone varieties where you placed a transparent film on it with your illustrations and they were magnified on a screen. This could reach a larger audience, but was still limited in you had to have all of your illustrations lined up and ready to go. This was good for discussions as you could use a marker on blank sheets to record audience responses.

Another old fashioned method of illustrating your message was the slide projector. Many of those who grew up in church should remember the missionaries who augmented their talk with slides of what they did and the people they were working with. As the speaker talked, you could hear the click and whir of the projector as he or she advanced through their presentation.

Today our laptop computers, software and a led projector have largely done away with white boards, overhead and slide projectors.

Many modern illustrating tools available to a speaker may include a scanner which acts like an overhead. The speaker can place a piece of paper or even a book on the scan and it will project it through the computer to a projector.

The smartboard combines the old fashioned white board with technology which allows the speaker to write on it, project a presentation or with a digital pen write comments directly on the board through the computer.

Handouts

Growing up in a church family which was attached to a Bible college was a unique experience. We were often given handouts by the speaker with his outline or supplementary material. What I thought was a normal part of Church culture turned out to be an exception. Handouts are rarely used in most Churches.

Handouts can be very good visuals especially for smaller groups. You can create supplementary material for your audience to examine later, for further study or facts and figures which you wanted your audience to remember. I still think homework should be the norm; give your audience something to encourage them to get into the Word when they walk out the door on Sunday mornings.

A handout could contain your outline so people can follow you and take notes. It is harder to do this with a larger congregation as you have to take time to have several people handing them out while you start your introduction or get your outline in to the church secretary early enough to include it in the bulletins. That is only good until the bulletins run out.

If part of your delivery is to initiate a discussion or to do a Bible study, then handouts are very helpful. You can divide your audience into groups to work through the questions and then come back together to report on their findings.

Software

When it comes to software packages the undisputed king is PowerPoint. This versatile program is the electronic version of a slide show and is the most commonly used program for creating effective visuals. There are other programs which do the same thing, such as Open Office's Impress or Corel's Presentations, but PowerPoint is the more well-known one.

There are some important things to keep in mind when you are designing a presentation. The first one is to not go crazy with all the different effects which can be accomplished with a few clicks of your mouse. It will make for a confusing presentation which will have a negative impact on your audience. If you use effects, use them sparingly and for purposes like bring up one bulleted point at a time.

You also want to avoid cramming your entire message on one slide. No one will read it. Remember you are using your presentation as a visual aid for your message. If you want to handout copies of your sermon, then you need to find a photocopier. Keep your text limited from four to six lines and a maximum of 40 words. This includes using bulleted points.

You should use a san-serif font style. Most fonts fall into two categories; serif and san-serif. Serifs are the little tails you see on the ends of letters. For example, **Times New Roman** is a serif text. The font used to write this study guide – **Calibri** is san-serif. San-serif fonts are easier to read in a visual presentation.

It is also important to remember the size of the font. In most cases you are going to be projected to your audience on a screen and people in the back of the room need to read it. If you use a small font size, such as 11 point which is the font in this book, people will have a hard time reading it. For readability purposes use a font size of around 24. Also make sure you are contrasting your type color with the background. Use light colored text on a dark background or vice-versa. If your text and background are similar in lightness or darkness it will be hard to read.

You can use more decorative fonts for your headlines, but choose those which are easily read. Fonts such as *Blackadder ITC* or Chiller are more difficult to read than say **Arial Black** or **Cooper Black.**

Keep your slides consistent by using the slide master feature of PowerPoint. Although you could (and should!) vary the columns, points, pictures, etc. consistent backgrounds help to unify your presentation.

Aligning your text to the left or right is more pleasing to the eye than centered text. Also keep in mind less is more. If you overload your slide with text or images you will confuse and lose your audience.

Images are one of those things which can be very good or very bad. You will find arguments from they add visual interest and engage your audience to they are distracting and annoying.

The middle ground is to use images only if they add important information or help make an abstract concept clearer. Images include pictures, clip art, graphs and charts. Any visual element you are considering including in your presentation should be used with illustrating your points and supporting your argument.

The same advice goes for audio or video files as well. You can embed a link to a web page or file into your presentation which will play on command or automatically when the slide is displayed.

The principle "less is more" also applies to the length of your presentation. A rule of thumb is to limit your presentation to about 10 slides. If you need to go longer, then you are no longer preaching, but giving a lecture. Well, not really but if you have to create a longer slide presentation, work in a break of some kind, like a review or discussion to help keep your audience focused. A rule of thumb is to use one slide per minute. You can leave your slide up for longer than a minute, or even less than a minute, but you risk losing your audience if you overwhelm them with a flurry of slides or putting them to sleep by never changing your slide.

Other software which is not used as much in preaching includes programs like Media Player or ITunes to present audio or video clips. Appropriate images or a song can have a great impact when it compliments your message.

Online Tools

Just because you don't have PowerPoint doesn't mean you don't have that opportunity to create effective visuals for your message. There are a wide variety of online tools which can help you with your presentation. Many of them are free to use. Online web tools like Prezzi.com, Wikispaces.com and cloud technology can be a great help when planning your message.

If you are planning a Bible study for instance you can put your notes on the cloud with web tools like Google Drive, or ICloud to share with other people in your study. Wikis are collaborative Web sites which allow for multiple participants to edit documents, leave messages and other activities which would make conducting an online study much easier. If you gave your audience access to your messages or leave homework for them online, you would have an audience which is involved in your message before you even preach it. Or they may decide not to come to church as they have already seen your message…

With all of the tools we have discussed it is important to keep in mind they are not substitutes for preaching. You still need to create a message which will engage your audience. A poorly crafted message will not be helped by good visuals any more than a top notch sermon benefits from poor visual aids.

One last piece of advice; have a plan B. If you are using technology as part of your presentation arsenal, keep in mind, stuff happens and you may not have access to your presentation or other illustrations you have planned.

For the practice

Choose one of the outlines we have been working on throughout this book and develop visuals for it. Create a handout and a visual presentation, either using software on your computer or online tools.

If you are looking for more information on creating effective visuals, repeat after me: "Google is my friend."

Lesson Eight

Delivering Your Message

You have put your time in. The research is as complete as you can make it. You have developed a killer outline which is spot on and supports your thesis. You have your illustrations ready to go and created a PowerPoint to wow your audience's socks off. You are ready to go.

Almost.

You are a vital component to the effectiveness of your message. From the tone of your voice, to your physical appearance to your body language all contribute to the success of your message. You now get to stand up in front of a group of people to share what God has laid on your heart with your message. But you only have a few minutes to capture and keep their attention.

When delivering your message there are some very important steps to consider when you open your mouth. They consist of getting your audience's attention, build credibility and preview your message.

If this sounds familiar, it should as we discussed this in the chapter covering planning your message. If you don't remember that... then you need to go back and review it: you either have a very short memory or you skipped over that chapter.

First Impressions

From the moment you step up to the podium, pulpit or whatever you step up to you are under scrutiny and the audience begins to evaluate whether or not they should buy into and consider your message. The moment starts from the moment they see you. It takes less than a tenth of a second to begin forming a first impression.

Even the clothing your wear can be distracting. I remember a beginning preacher who had no idea about coordinating his outfit. So he would wear plaid pants with striped ties and shirts festooned with polka-dots... all at the same time. He was a pretty good preacher even in his early years, but people rarely talked about his message. They discussed his outfits. Perhaps because this was in the 70's; the era of the loud polyester leisure suit, which may have something to do with it.

Fortunately he got married and his wife made sure he was dressed properly. Loud splashy outfits do not enhance your message. They detract from it.

I'm not saying you should wear a suit and tie every time you get up to preach, although some congregations expect that of their preachers. You should choose your wardrobe so that your message is highlighted and not you. It should also mirror the general appearances of the people listening to you. If you are speaking at an informal fellowship, then you can probably skip the suit coat and tie. Many churches on Sunday mornings no longer require the preacher to be in a suit, but you perhaps should be a bit more formal than cargo shorts and sandals topped off with your favorite branded t-shirt. Unless of course your audience is a group of teens at a youth retreat.

Credibility

Now with that all-important first impression out of the way, we can turn to the next part of the delivery; establishing your credibility.

In the lesson on planning you message we did not discuss a great deal about building your credibility. It is almost contradictory as you are there to represent God and your authority comes from the Word. Now if you are familiar with the audience, this is not as an important issue as if you were addressing a new audience.

Before you dive into your message, you should provide assurance you are the subject matter expert (SME). Although you are trying to keep your knees from knocking together and have been praying someone remembers to put a glass of water on the pulpit because your tongue is sticking to the roof of your mouth, you are the SME for the next 30-45 minutes.

As you present your credentials, which may as simple as "In my studies in the Bible this past week or so..." you are also tying in your credentials with the purpose of your presentation. In doing so you are tying in your interests in with the interest of your audience. You are implying your audience will be interested in what you have discovered.

Voice

The next thing to consider when you speak is your voice. Many a sermon was killed off by a person speaking too softly, too loudly, or the more dreaded monotone, which is a sure way to lose your audience as you have lulled them into a mental stupor from where they will not return.

When you are delivering your message, think of it as having a conversation with your audience. You want to modulate the tone of your voice, raise and lower it as you speak and speak at a reasonable rate, not too fast or slow. If you have issues with this then the key is to practice your message and record your voice. Yeah, I know most people have an aversion to hearing their own voice. Think how your audience feels?

Listening to your messages will help you to pinpoint potential issues where you may distract your audience.

You want to choose wording that is familiar to your audience. Unless you are an academic addressing your peers or a theology professor, you want to engage your audience and not disengage them with words they have to look up in a dictionary to understand.

Facial Expression

Along with talking, your face should also be expressive when you speak. You facial features should mirror your message. Smile or make a funny face if needed. Don't stand gripping the sides of the pulpit so hard your finger prints are etched into it. And don't present your sermon with a poker face. We want to reach our audience and making your facial expressions match your message will go a long way into engaging your audience and assist them in accepting your argument.

There are many times I have wanted to challenge a preacher on their message as they stood in the pulpit because their tone of voice and facial expressions appear not to agree with their message. You have to preach it like you mean it.

> Pastor George thought he had really made a connection with his congregation that morning. They seemed to be electrified and took more than usual interest.
>
> After the message, he discovered some people thought he had dropped an "f-bomb." It led to a rather lively conversation after the service
>
> (McVey)

Body Language

Like your face your body will also convey a lot of information about what you are feeling or attempting to conceal. I had a teacher who when he was teaching would constantly fiddle with his tie. It was an unconscious action which was distracting to his students. A minister who constantly rubs his nose or ear, or paces may be projecting feelings of nervousness to their audience. The audience will pick up on this nervousness and also start to exhibit the same anxiety

When I am teaching, I will often carry a marker, or pen in my hand when I am speaking. It helps me to concentrate on my message and releases some of my nervous energy. I also like to pace from one side of the podium as I talk and make eye contact with my audience. I do not recommend only standing behind the pulpit, placing your hands on the edges and delivering your message without moving. People will quickly zone out. Body language helps you to convey your message and show people you believe what you are preaching.

Reduce the Anxiety

One of the biggest obstacles in successfully delivering your message is your own levels of anxiety at the thought of standing up in front of a group of people and preaching. It doesn't matter whether it's your first time or you have been speaking for years. Those feelings don't totally go away. You may have a killer message, but your nerves get the better of you and you forget everything. That is why you carry cheat notes with you, either a typed (or written) outline on paper or index cards you can carry with you. If your church has a projector which faces the rear of the auditorium you can project your notes from there.

First and foremost, and it should go without saying, but then people don't remember to do this, is pray. Spend some time alone with God before you step into that pulpit. Ask for His guidance and grace as you bring what He has laid on your heart. Ask for the Holy Spirit to prepare not only you as the messenger but also for the audience who will be receiving this message. Praying taps into God's power.

You are not perfect, so don't expect your preaching to be perfect either. You are sharing what you feel God has led you to share with your audience. You are the vessel and He will use you if you allow Him.

Along with that piece of information is the need to practice your message. In front of a mirror, walking around, while you are waiting at the stop light, take every opportunity to run through your message and getting your points down.

Before you get up on the stage, remember to breathe. Breathing deeply and consciously helps you to focus your mind and relax your body. Aim to feel comfortable when you stand behind that pulpit. Focus on your message and your audience when you are speaking. If your mind is on that, then you are not thinking about you and making yourself more nervous.

If you find you are getting anxious or you notice your audience is starting to mentally leave, take what is called a "three-second break." Pause to take a drink of water, check the outline for where you are in your delivery and give the audience a bit of time to absorb your point before moving on. This may seem to go against your nature and the idea of wanting to get it over with, but the occasional pause will go a long way to keep you on track and your audience with you.

Have a plan B when you get up to speak. Be prepared when the computer decides not to speak to the projector or the light burns out, the sound system crashes or the lights go out. Every preacher has been there and even when things don't go according to your plan, they are going according to God's. So keep on going – the finish line is still straight ahead regardless of the hurdles you have to jump.

Finish Strong

Remember earlier in this study when preparing your outline to stick to three steps: Tell them what you are going to tell them, tell them and tell them what you told them? During your delivery you should have been leading your audience to your conclusion. So many sermons fall at this point because the preacher did not have a clear objective.

Summarize your message in your conclusion and highlight your arguments. Deliver your challenge to them and emphasize what you want them to take away from this message. Many churches offer some sort of response avenues such as coming to the front for prayer. One of the purposes of God's Word is to change lives. Show them what God wants to change in their lives and the next steps.

An important step in closing your message is closing in prayer. Commit your message, the audience and yourself to God. You have done your job and now it is time for the Holy Spirit to do His. When you are finished, thank your audience for taking the time to stick with you to the end, gather up your notes or other material, leave the stage and meet and greet the congregation. Take time to take a deep breath and relax.

Congratulations! You did it.

Lesson Nine

Evaluating Your Message

Now that you have reached your goal of preaching a sermon you want to know how well you did. Unfortunately most people will not be honest with you.

Resist the temptation to ask people how you did. It is awkward for both of you – they will not want to hurt your feelings, especially if you are asking friends and family.

If you are looking for feedback, then ask several people ahead of time. Give them a sermon outline or rubric to make notes on as you speak and gather them up afterward. Choose people whom you don't necessarily know, such as your besties, although you can throw one or two in for comparison. Keep them anonymous so people will feel more comfortable especially if they are providing negative feedback.

A Rubric is another evaluation tool which shows the elements needed to reach the goal and how well you did. I have included a sample which I adapted when I evaluated oral presentations for a Business Communication class.

You can also take a video of yourself preaching. A video recording will show you things which you may not be aware of, such as mannerisms which may be distracting. Although we are inundated with an obsession with selfies and self-promotion, many are uncomfortable watching or listening to themselves. Often people don't like the sound of their voices being that what they are hearing recorded is not what they normally hear when they speak.

Just as writers are encouraged to be readers, preachers should also be good listeners to other preachers. Take notes and evaluate the speaker and his or her message. Don't limit yourself to just your own circle of acquaintances but listen to a variety of preachers. The more you listen to other preachers, the better you will become at delivering your own message.

On Sunday mornings and evenings you will normally find me in church with my Bible and a notebook. This is a habit I started as a teen and have continued. Recently I was cleaning out a box of stuff and came across notebooks I kept of sermons over 30 years ago. Now I'm not recommending you do the same. But note keeping is beneficial in that it helps you to remember what the preacher was talking about. For many of them, I remember the circumstances of when and where those messages took place. Some of those speakers were just starting their careers at the time. Some of them are no longer with us, but some are and still actively preaching.

The worksheets at the end of this chapter include evaluation tools for you to use when listening to sermons or to hand out to people to evaluate your message when it is your turn to speak. Don't be afraid of evaluating your messages. It is a way to improve your speaking skills.

I am planning to have additional files loaded on my website which you can download and use for your personal use. The site is bibleschooldropout.com

God bless you as you undertake this important ministry.

Preaching Rubric

Date:

Name:

Topic:

Length:

	5	4	3	2	1
Presentation Skills	Enthusiastic, clear and engaging with all members of the audience	Enthusiastic, and engaging but sometimes unclear or some members not included	Enthusiastic but unable to maintain class attention throughout the presentation	Attempt made but lack of enthusiasm and unable to maintain attention throughout	------
Information Presented	Salient Points were clear and well supported with examples. Information was relevant	Salient points were made but sometimes unclear. Some Irrelevant information included.	Few key points were addressed and/or information lacked focus	Information presented was irrelevant or unrelated	------
Timing	Good timing	Timing to short or too long	Timing was too short or too long - pace was too fast or too slow	------	-------
Visual aids	PowerPoint, handout, and activity	PowerPoint, handout or activity	PowerPoint only	Included a handout or an activity	Did not include a visual aid

Comments:

Preaching Rubric

Date:

Name:

Topic:

Length:

	5	4	3	2	1
Presentation Skills	Enthusiastic, clear and engaging with all members of the audience	Enthusiastic, and engaging but sometimes unclear or some members not included	Enthusiastic but unable to maintain class attention throughout the presentation	Attempt made but lack of enthusiasm and unable to maintain class attention throughout	------
Information Presented	Salient Points were clear and well supported with examples. Information was relevant	Salient points were made but sometimes unclear. Some Irrelevant information included.	Few key points were addressed and/or information lacked focus	Information presented was irrelevant or unrelated	------
Timing	Good timing	Timing to short or too long	Timing was too short or too long - pace was too fast or too slow	------	-------
Visual aids	PowerPoint, handout, and activity	PowerPoint, handout or activity	PowerPoint only	Included a handout or an activity	Did not include a visual aid

Comments:

Preaching Rubric

Date:

Name:

Topic:

Length:

	5	4	3	2	1
Presentation Skills	Enthusiastic, clear and engaging with all members of the audience	Enthusiastic, and engaging but sometimes unclear or some members not included	Enthusiastic but unable to maintain class attention throughout the presentation	Attempt made but lack of enthusiasm and unable to maintain class attention throughout	------
Information Presented	Salient Points were clear and well supported with examples. Information was relevant	Salient points were made but sometimes unclear. Some Irrelevant information included.	Few key points were addressed and/or information lacked focus	Information presented was irrelevant or unrelated	------
Timing	Good timing	Timing to short or too long	Timing was too short or too long - pace was too fast or too slow	------	-------
Visual aids	PowerPoint, handout, and activity	PowerPoint, handout or activity	PowerPoint only	Included a handout or an activity	Did not include a visual aid

Comments:

Preaching Rubric

Date:

Name:

Topic:

Length:

	5	4	3	2	1
Presentation Skills	Enthusiastic, clear and engaging with all members of the audience	Enthusiastic, and engaging but sometimes unclear or some members not included	Enthusiastic but unable to maintain class attention throughout the presentation	Attempt made but lack of enthusiasm and unable to maintain class attention throughout	------
Information Presented	Salient Points were clear and well supported with examples. Information was relevant	Salient points were made but sometimes unclear. Some Irrelevant information included.	Few key points were addressed and/or information lacked focus	Information presented was irrelevant or unrelated	------
Timing	Good timing	Timing to short or too long	Timing was too short or too long - pace was too fast or too slow	------	-------
Visual aids	PowerPoint, handout, and activity	PowerPoint, handout or activity	PowerPoint only	Included a handout or an activity	Did not include a visual aid

Comments:

Sermon Notes

Speaker:	Date:	Location :
Scripture:	Title:	
Theme: (Purpose or goal of the message)		

Verse:	Point:	Message Notes:	Reference:

Takeaway:

Sermon Notes

Speaker:	Date:		Location :
Scripture:	Title:		
Theme: (Purpose or goal of the message)			
Verse:	Point:	Message Notes:	Reference:
Takeaway:			

Sermon Notes

Speaker:		Date:	Location :
Scripture:		Title:	
Theme: (Purpose or goal of the message)			
Verse:	Point:	Message Notes:	Reference:
Takeaway:			

Sermon Notes

Speaker:	Date:	Location :
Scripture:	Title:	
Theme: (Purpose or goal of the message)		

Verse:	Point:	Message Notes:	Reference:

Takeaway:

Additional Notes:

Resources

Websites:

There are a lot of sites on the web these days which offer assistance to up and coming preachers. Whether you are looking for examples to analyze or ideas for your next message, you will find what you are looking for. Just a word of caution however, please be careful when perusing the websites. Find out what they are about, what they believe and what they practice. The organization may have some weird and wonderful things which don't relate to Christianity. When I was doing tech support my favorite saying was "Google is my friend." It still is.

Bibleschooldropout.com

Churchleaders.com

Executableoutlines.com

Precept.org

Sermoncentral.com

Sermonaudio.com

Walkintheword.com

Books:

For those who still prefer actually reading a real book, (well you can get a lot of them online as well) here are some of the ones I recommend for further study. Some of them are classics and maybe hard to find.

Homiletics:

Blackwood, Andrew Watterson. Doctrinal Preaching for Today. Abingdon Press, Nashville, 1956

Broadus, John A. On the Preparation and Delivery of Sermons, 4th Ed. Hzrper and Row Publishers. 1979

Gibbs, Alfred P. The Preacher and His Preaching, Walterick Publishers, Kansas City

Robinson, Haddon W. Biblical Preaching: The Development and Delivery of Expository Messages. Baker Book House, Grand Rapids. 1980

MacDonald, James, Preaching: 25 Things You Can't Learn in School. Walk in the Word, Elgin, 2007

Pelton, Randal E. Preaching With Accuracy. Kregel Publications, Grand Rapids. 2014

Bible Study:

Arthur, Kay. How to Study Your Bible, Harvest House, Eugene, 1994

Olar, Stephen. The Bible School Dropout's Bigger and Better Guide to Bible Study. Bible School Dropout Publications. Sault Ste. Marie, 2008

Olar, Stephen. The Bible School Dropout's Guide to More Bible Study. Bible School Dropout Publications, Sault Ste. Marie. 2010

Hermeneutics:

Berkhof, L. Principles of Biblical Interpretation, Baker Book House. Grand Rapids. 1950

Carson, D.A., Woodbridge, John D. Eds. Hermeneutics, Authority and the Canon. Academie Books/ Zondervan Publishing House, Grand Rapids. 1986

Ramm, Bernard, Protestant Biblical Interpretation, 3rd. ed. Baker Book House. Grand Rapids. 1970

Christian Education:

Eavey, C.B. Principles of Teaching for Christian Teachers, Zondervan Publishing House, Grand Rapids. 1940

Gregory, John Milton. The Seven Laws of Teaching. Baker Book House. Grand Rapids. 1954

Wilkinson, Bruce. The Seven Laws of the Learner: Applied Principles of Learning. Walk Thru the Bible Ministries. Atlanta. 1988

Speaking:

Toastmasters International - www.toastmasters.org

Works Cited

Blackwood, Andrew Watterson. *Doctrinal Preaching for Today*. New York: Abingdon Press, 1956.

Broadus, John A. *On the Preparation and Delivery of Sermons, 4th ed.* San Fransico: Harper and Row, Publishers, 1979.

—. *On the Prepartion and Delivery of Sermons, 4th ed.* . San Franciso: Harper and Row Publishers, 1979.

Copeland, Mark. "Moral Issues Confronting Christians." 2009. *executableoutlines.com.* pdf. 30 06 2015.

Gibbs, Alfred P. *The Preacher and His Preaching*. Kansas City: Walterick Publishers, unknown.

—. *The Preacher and His Preaching*. Kansas City: Walterick Publishers, n/a.

—. *The Preacher and His Preaching, 6th ed.* Kansas City: Walterick Publishers, n/a .

http://dictionary.reference.com/browse/sermon?s=t.
"http://dictionary.reference.com/browse/sermon?s=t." 09 06 2015. *dictionary.com.* web. 09 06 2015.

McVey, George Sr. *Personal notes* Stephen Olar. 2015.

Morgan, R. J. *Nelson's Complete Book of Stories, Illustrations and Quotes*. Nashville, 2000. electronic ed.

Olar, Stephen. *The Bible School Dropout's Bigger and Better Guide to Bible Study*. Sault Ste. Marie: Bible School Dropout Publications, 2008.

—. *The Bible School Dropout's Bigger and Better Guide to Bible Study*. Sault Ste. Marie: Bible School Dropout Publications, 2008.

—. *The Bible School Dropout's Guide to More Bible Study*. Sault Ste. Marie: Bible School Dropout Publications, 2010.

Ramm, Bernard. *Protestanct Biblical Interpretation, Third Revised Edition*. Ann Arbor: Baker Book House Company, 1970.

Robinson, Haddon W. *Biblical Preaching*. Grand Rapids: Baker Book House, 1980.

Thill, John V, Catherine L Bovee and Ava Cross. *Excellence in Business Communication; Fourth Canadian Edition*. Toronto: Pearson, 2015.

About the Author

Hi, I'm the author *of The Bible School Dropout's Bigger and Better Guide to Bible Study*, *The Bible School Dropout's Guide to More Bible Study*, *Xtreme Xianity*, *Core Elements*, *In Hot Pursuit* and The Name of the Lord is series. I am also the author of the novels *Free* and *Icthus*.

My Bible studies are based upon inductive Bible study methods which use grammatical-historical, normal or literal methods of interpretation. If you can ask the questions; who, what, where, why, when and how, then you can do an inductive Bible study.

I really am a Bible school dropout. I left Bible school at the beginning of my third year. But that was not the end of my Christian experience and I have been actively teaching and preaching for over 30 years.

It doesn't matter if you have had formal training or not. Anyone with the right tools and practice can study their Bible for themselves. I encourage people to learn how to study their Bibles and learn what it has to say instead of letting others tell them what it says.

I can be reached at bibleschooldropout@gmail.com. You can also visit my website www.bibleschooldropout.com.

www.ingramcontent.com/pod-product-compliance
Lightning Source LLC
Chambersburg PA
CBHW081153090426
42736CB00017B/3309